Contents

Written by Rachael Davis

Illustrated by Christian Cornia

Collins

What is fear?

Fear is how we feel when we are **afraid** we might come to harm.

What do you fear?

You might fear a bee ...   the dark ...

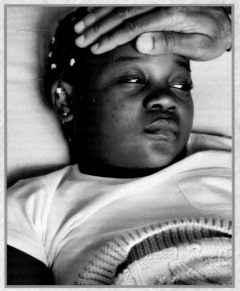

getting sick ...

or failing a test.

You might be afraid to go up high ...

or join a crowd.

Fight or flight

When you feel fear, your brain might tell you to get cross, stand still or run!

Fight or flight is an **instinct** that is in us all.

Fight or flight is in animals too, from fish to cats to cows.

Is fear bad?

A bit of fear can be good. We need some fear to keep us from harm.

But too much fear can hurt.

How to fight fear

Fears come and go.

It can help if you stand up to your fear.

How can you stand up to fear?

13

Step 1: Point it out

Fear can feel hard and **spoil** your fun.

Tell an adult or a pal how you feel. It might help.

15

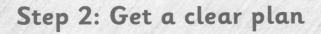

Step 2: Get a clear plan

Fight your fear step by step. Now you can turn your fear into a goal.

Aim high and ...

Step 3: Do not fear fear!

We all feel afraid now and then, and that is all right.

But do not let fears limit you.

Glossary

afraid feel fear

flight to run from a thing

instinct a need to act

spoil to turn good into bad

Index

Fight fear!

all sorts of fears

fight or flight

22

After reading

Letters and Sounds: Phases 3 and 4

Word count: 232

Focus phonemes: /ch/ /sh/ /th/ /ng/ /ai/ /ee/ /igh/ /oa/ /oo/ /oo/ /ar/ /or/ /ur/ /ow/ /oi/ /ear/, and adjacent consonants

Common exception words: of, to, the, go, into, all, by, are, we, be, you, do, some, come, when, out, what, your

Curriculum links: PSHE: Mental health

National Curriculum learning objectives: Reading/word reading: apply phonic knowledge and skills as the route to decode words; read accurately by blending sounds in unfamiliar words containing GPCs that have been taught; read common exception words, noting unusual correspondences between spelling and sound and where these occur in words; Reading/comprehension (KS2): understand what they read, in books they can read independently, by checking that the text makes sense to them, discussing their understanding and explaining the meaning of words in context; by drawing inferences such as inferring characters' feelings, thoughts and motives from their actions

Developing fluency

- Read the book together, taking turns to read a double page.
- Demonstrate reading dramatically to bring out the contrasting moods of fear and determination.

Phonic practice

- Practise reading words with adjacent consonants:
  instinct   flight   brain   adult   spoil   afraid
- Challenge your child to find and read all the words with adjacent consonants on page 14. (*step, point, hard, spoil, adult, help*)

Extending vocabulary

- Compare the girl on page 11 with the children on page 19. Ask your child to think of as many words as they can to describe how the children might be feeling.

  page 11 (e.g. *worried, scared*)   page 19 (e.g. *powerful, confident*)